DWELL

A Study Guide

FOR EXPANDED SCRIPTURE MEMORY

· · · · · · · · · · ·

BELOVED BIBLE PASSAGES

The Beatitudes (Matthew 5:1-12)
Christian Love (1 Corinthians 13)
The Armor of God (Ephesians 6:10-20)
The Lord's Prayer (Matthew 6:5-15)
The Fruit of the Spirit (Galatians 5:16-26)
The Great Commission (Matthew 28:18-20)

Scripture memory is an incredibly valuable discipline for Christians. We can memorize single verses, or we can memorize longer sections of Scripture. Many of us have probably memorized individual verses before, but taking on a longer passage of Scripture may be intimidating. The Dwell Study Guide focuses on memorizing longer passages of Scripture. While it is not realistic for most of us to memorize the entire Bible word-for-word, there is great value to memorizing longer passages of Scripture. Whether it is a key section of Scripture, one chapter of a book, or even an entire book of the Bible, this type of Scripture memory can be greatly beneficial and edifying for Christians.

Memorizing larger sections of Scripture can help us to better learn, understand, and remember the context and message of the Bible as a whole all the way down to its individual verses. In addition to this, when we have taken the time to meditate and memorize sections of Scripture, we can better recall them in the times we need them most. Whether we want to articulate the message of the gospel well and in its intended context or provide hope and comfort to ourself or others, investing in knowing and remembering God's Word will reap the benefits of storing this truth in our hearts.

The inspiration and purpose for the Dwell Study Guide can be summed up in Colossians 3:16, which says, "Let the word of Christ dwell richly among you, in all wisdom teaching and admonishing one another through psalms, hymns, and spiritual songs, singing to God with gratitude in your hearts."

We want to daily pursue a deeper knowledge and understanding of God's Word so that we can continually dwell more and more on the truth of the promises found in Scripture. God's Word is precious, and yet it's easy for us to become unappreciative, complacent, and even apathetic toward Scripture, in part because of how easily accessible it is to us. Many of us have multiple copies of the Bible in our language, not to mention apps and websites where we can access the Bible as well. The access we have to Scripture is a blessing, to be sure, but it is not one that we should take for granted. Do not let how easily accessible Scripture is to you keep you from the practice of memorizing and dwelling on God's Word. Our access to Scripture should spur us on to know it more, allowing that deepened knowledge to transform our hearts and lives.

Do not be intimidated by Scripture memory! Our guide will walk you through one verse at a time, while providing helpful study information such as book introductions, context of passages, and word studies to enrich the memorization process and help you to dwell on the truth of Scripture. We don't want you to simply focus on or become overwhelmed by the process of memorization itself. The goal is not a head knowledge of Scripture that you can recite on demand; the goal is to know God more and dwell on who He is by seeking to know and understand His Word better.

We all know there are so many things competing for our attention in this life. But we promise you that time spent in God's Word, deepening your knowledge for the purpose of knowing God more and allowing that to transform your heart and mind, will never be a waste of time. This is something worth prioritizing, and we hope this guide is a useful tool in approaching Scripture memory in a clear and purposeful way.

Recommendations
TO AID IN SCRIPTURE MEMORY

We will provide a starting point for working through memorizing a larger passage of Scripture (whether a chapter or a key section), breaking it down verse by verse. You can go at whatever pace works best for your life—whether that is a verse a day, a verse a week, or something in between. You could consider this guide as the foundation to your Scripture memorization. In addition to this, you can add other methods throughout the day to further aid in your memorization. This can be customized to fit your learning style, using techniques to best help you remember a particular verse or passage throughout the day. Below are a few additional methods to aid in memorization.

 ## LISTEN

Many phone apps and websites provide a free audio version of the Bible. You could listen to the entirety of the passage you are memorizing a few times a day to further aid memorization and remind yourself of the whole passage even though you might be focused on studying only one of the verses on any given day or week.

 ## WRITE IT OUT

Write the verse out in a journal, or on scratch paper, or on a white board multiple times a day. The repetition of writing the verse will aid in memory further than just the one time we provide a space for it per verse in the journal. Whether creative lettering is your thing or you just write it out in your regular handwriting, this is another great method for memorizing.

POST IT UP

This is a great method to use in conjunction with the write it out method. Whether you write out the day's verse on a sticky note or a notecard, post the written verse in places so you will be reminded of it throughout the day. Paste a sticky note on your fridge or your desk, or leave a note card by your front door or in your car. Whatever spots you see or pass by as you go about your day, place a written copy of the verse there as a reminder. A great step forward would be to print out the entirety of the passage you are memorizing and tape it up in a place near where you spend a more significant amount of time at some point during your day. Whether that is your bathroom mirror or a wall in your kitchen or on a bulletin board by your workspace, this a great way to keep the whole passage on your mind and read through it as a whole a few times a day.

SCREEN TIME

Take a picture or screenshot of the verse you are memorizing that day, and make it your screensaver on your phone. This will be a constant reminder to read and recite the verse a few times every time you pick up your phone.

DOODLE

If you like to draw or doodle, take a little time to sketch out some visuals that help you remember that day's verse. This is not for everyone, and it might work better for some verses more than others, but if you are a visual learner and enjoy drawing, this might be something that is helpful to mix in from time to time.

PRAYER

Incorporate the verses you are currently memorizing into prayers throughout the day as a way of keeping the words—and more importantly, their message—at the forefront of your mind.

AN INTRO TO
The Beatitudes
MATTHEW 5:1-12

The word *beatitude* is Latin for blessing. This ties in well as the name of this portion of Scripture because of the eight blessings highlighted in this passage. Jesus shared the Beatitudes as an introduction to the well-known Sermon on the Mount in Matthew 5. The Sermon on the Mount teaches that Jesus is not about empty and ritualistic practices but desires to see changed hearts that respond out of love and worship. The Beatitudes introduce this well by highlighting attitudes of the heart that were contrary to what was deemed valuable at that time by Christian culture. This is precisely the corrective intent when Jesus spoke to his original audience. Jesus originally shared this message with His disciples, but it is also meant for Jesus' disciples today.

We can glean wisdom from this passage, reminded of those truly worthy of a blessing in God's eyes—the poor in spirit, those who mourn, the humble, those who hunger and thirst for righteousness, the merciful, the pure in heart, the peacemakers, and those who are persecuted because of righteousness. Though the world may not see those things as rewarding, this passage reminds us that we can wait with hope because our reward will be great in heaven.

Preparation
FOR MEMORIZING MATTHEW 5:1-12

 READ MATTHEW 5:1-12

 WRITE OUT MATTHEW 5:1-12
on the lines provided below

_____

_____

_____

_____

_____

_____

_____

_____

_____

_____

_____

_____

_____

_____

_____

_____

_____

_____

_____

_____

_____

_____

_____

_____

_____

_____

_____

_____

_____

_____

_____

_____

_____

_____

_____

 PRAY *over the upcoming time you will spend memorizing and meditating on Matthew 5:1-12*

Matthew 5:1

🤚 **PRAY** *for your time in Scripture memory today*

📖 **READ MATTHEW 5:1** *ten times*

> When he saw the crowds, he went up on the mountain, and after he sat down, his disciples came to him.

Matthew 5:1

📢 **RECITE MATTHEW 5:1** *ten times*

✏️ **WRITE OUT MATTHEW 5:1**
on the lines provided below

_____

_____

_____

_____

_____

_____

Matthew 5:2

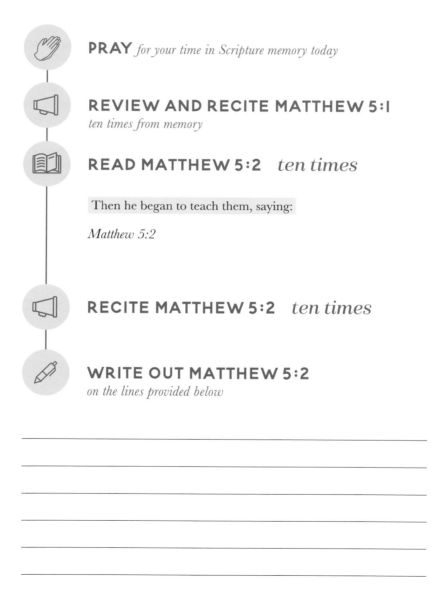

PRAY *for your time in Scripture memory today*

REVIEW AND RECITE MATTHEW 5:1
ten times from memory

READ MATTHEW 5:2   *ten times*

Then he began to teach them, saying:

Matthew 5:2

RECITE MATTHEW 5:2   *ten times*

WRITE OUT MATTHEW 5:2
on the lines provided below

Matthew 5:3

PRAY *for your time in Scripture memory today*

REVIEW AND RECITE
- *Recite Matthew 5:1 from memory once*
- *Review and recite Matthew 5:2 by memory ten times*

READ MATTHEW 5:3 *ten times*

"Blessed are the poor in spirit,

for the kingdom of heaven is theirs.

Matthew 5:3

RECITE MATTHEW 5:3 *ten times*

WRITE OUT MATTHEW 5:3
on the lines provided below

Matthew 5:4

PRAY *for your time in Scripture memory today*

REVIEW AND RECITE
- *Recite Matthew 5:1-2 from memory once*
- *Review and recite Matthew 5:3 by memory ten times*

READ MATTHEW 5:4 *ten times*

Blessed are those who mourn,

for they will be comforted.

Matthew 5:4

RECITE MATTHEW 5:4 *ten times*

WRITE OUT MATTHEW 5:4
on the lines provided below

Matthew 5:5

PRAY *for your time in Scripture memory today*

REVIEW AND RECITE
- *Recite Matthew 5:1-3 from memory once*
- *Review and recite Matthew 5:4 by memory ten times*

READ MATTHEW 5:5 *ten times*

Blessed are the humble,

for they will inherit the earth.

Matthew 5:5

RECITE MATTHEW 5:5 *ten times*

WRITE OUT MATTHEW 5:5
on the lines provided below

A Word Study
FOR MATTHEW 5:1-12

μακάριος
---
makarios

USED 50 TIMES

DEFINITION
blessed, happy

μακάριος

The Greek word *makarios* is translated into English meaning blessed or happy. It is used fifty times in the Bible and nine times in the Beatitudes. This word highlights the theme of blessings found in Matthew 5:1-12. In Christ, we see the blessing that results from walking in obedience and faith in accordance with God's commands. When we walk in a manner worthy of that which we have been called to as Christians, we are blessed beyond measure. But our blessings do not look like earthly riches; instead, they look like the comfort of Christ, the mercy of Christ, the fullness of Christ, and an abundant reward secured in heaven which is far more valuable and lasting than any earthly thing.

Matthew 5:6

PRAY *for your time in Scripture memory today*

REVIEW AND RECITE
- *Recite Matthew 5:1-4 from memory once*
- *Review and recite Matthew 5:5 by memory ten times*

READ MATTHEW 5:6 *ten times*

Blessed are those who hunger and thirst for righteousness, for they will be filled.

Matthew 5:6

RECITE MATTHEW 5:6 *ten times*

WRITE OUT MATTHEW 5:6
on the lines provided below

_____

_____

_____

_____

_____

_____

Matthew 5:7

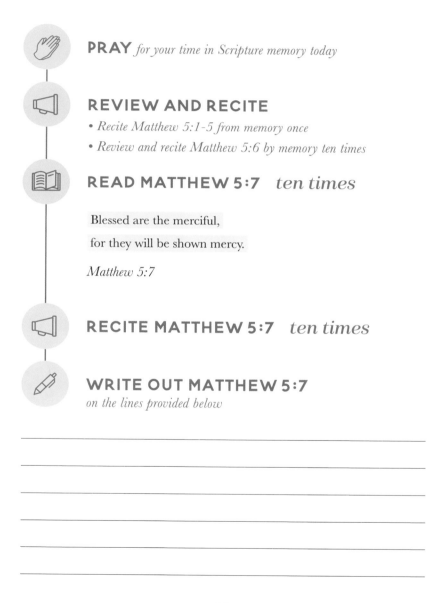

PRAY *for your time in Scripture memory today*

REVIEW AND RECITE
- *Recite Matthew 5:1-5 from memory once*
- *Review and recite Matthew 5:6 by memory ten times*

READ MATTHEW 5:7 *ten times*

Blessed are the merciful,

for they will be shown mercy.

Matthew 5:7

RECITE MATTHEW 5:7 *ten times*

WRITE OUT MATTHEW 5:7
on the lines provided below

Matthew 5:8

PRAY *for your time in Scripture memory today*

REVIEW AND RECITE
- *Recite Matthew 5:1-6 from memory once*
- *Review and recite Matthew 5:7 by memory ten times*

READ MATTHEW 5:8 *ten times*

Blessed are the pure in heart,

for they will see God.

Matthew 5:8

RECITE MATTHEW 5:8 *ten times*

WRITE OUT MATTHEW 5:8
on the lines provided below

Matthew 5:9

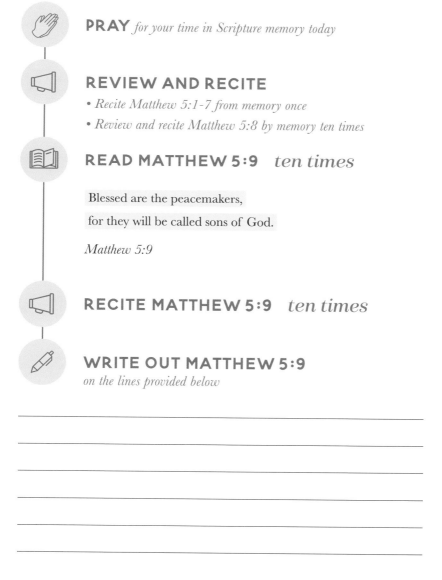

PRAY *for your time in Scripture memory today*

REVIEW AND RECITE
- *Recite Matthew 5:1-7 from memory once*
- *Review and recite Matthew 5:8 by memory ten times*

READ MATTHEW 5:9 *ten times*

Blessed are the peacemakers,

for they will be called sons of God.

Matthew 5:9

RECITE MATTHEW 5:9 *ten times*

WRITE OUT MATTHEW 5:9
on the lines provided below

Matthew 5:10

PRAY *for your time in Scripture memory today*

REVIEW AND RECITE
- *Recite Matthew 5:1-8 from memory once*
- *Review and recite Matthew 5:9 by memory ten times*

READ MATTHEW 5:10 *ten times*

Blessed are those who are persecuted because of righteousness, for the kingdom of heaven is theirs.

Matthew 5:10

RECITE MATTHEW 5:10 *ten times*

WRITE OUT MATTHEW 5:10
on the lines provided below

Matthew 5:11

PRAY *for your time in Scripture memory today*

REVIEW AND RECITE
- *Recite Matthew 5:1-9 from memory once*
- *Review and recite Matthew 5:10 by memory ten times*

READ MATTHEW 5:11 *ten times*

> "You are blessed when they insult you and persecute you and falsely say every kind of evil against you because of me.
>
> *Matthew 5:11*

RECITE MATTHEW 5:11 *ten times*

WRITE OUT MATTHEW 5:11
on the lines provided below

_____

_____

_____

_____

_____

_____

Matthew 5:12

PRAY *for your time in Scripture memory today*

REVIEW AND RECITE
- *Recite Matthew 5:1-10 from memory once*
- *Review and recite Matthew 5:11 by memory ten times*

READ MATTHEW 5:12   *ten times*

Be glad and rejoice, because your reward is great in heaven.

For that is how they persecuted the prophets who were before you.

Matthew 5:12

RECITE MATTHEW 5:12   *ten times*

WRITE OUT MATTHEW 5:12
on the lines provided below

_____

_____

_____

_____

_____

_____

Conclusion

FOR MATTHEW 5:1-12 SCRIPTURE MEMORY

✏️ **WRITE OUT MATTHEW 5:1-12 FROM MEMORY**
on the lines provided below

_____

_____

_____

_____

_____

_____

_____

_____

_____

_____

_____

_____

_____

_____

_____

_____

_____

_____

_____

_____

_____

_____

_____

_____

_____

_____

_____

_____

_____

_____

_____

_____

_____

_____

_____

_____

_____

_____

 PRAY _through the passage you have just memorized, thanking God for His character and how He has allowed you to study and dwell on His Word during this time._

AN INTRO TO

1 Corinthians 13

CHRISTIAN LOVE

Right in the middle of Paul's teaching on spiritual gifts is the well-known chapter on love in 1 Corinthians 13. He emphasizes the importance of spiritual gifts, while also stating that without love, our gifts have little value. Love must be the primary motivation for how we use our gifts. Paul specifically mentions the gifts of tongues, prophecy, knowledge, faith, and giving. These gifts cannot accomplish their purpose without love at the forefront of our motives.

Additionally, Paul describes love and many of its attributes in this chapter. We get a picture of what love is and is not and how it should be reflected in our attitudes and lives. This is an important distinction to make in how we are to best show love to others. Jesus reminds us of the importance of showing love to one another in John 13:35 which reads, "By this everyone will know that you are my disciples, if you love one another." The call to love promotes unity and brotherhood among the body while serving as a gospel witness to a watching world. This is not only an encouragement given by the Apostle Paul but a command by God given to Christians to walk in love.

Preparation
FOR MEMORIZING I CORINTHIANS 13

 READ I CORINTHIANS 13

 **WRITE OUT I CORINTHIANS 13**
on the lines provided below

_____

_____

_____

_____

_____

_____

_____

_____

_____

_____

_____

_____

_____

_____

_____

_____

_____

_____

_____

_____

_____

_____

_____

_____

_____

_____

_____

_____

_____

_____

_____

_____

_____

_____

_____

_____

 PRAY *over the upcoming time you will spend memorizing and meditating on 1 Corinthians 13*

1 Corinthians 13:1

PRAY *for your time in Scripture memory today*

READ I CORINTHIANS 13:1 *ten times*

> If I speak human or angelic tongues but do not have love,
> I am a noisy gong or a clanging cymbal.

1 Corinthians 13:1

RECITE I CORINTHIANS 13:1 *ten times*

WRITE OUT I CORINTHIANS 13:1
on the lines provided below

1 Corinthians 13:2

PRAY *for your time in Scripture memory today*

REVIEW AND RECITE 1 CORINTHIANS 13:1
ten times from memory

READ 1 CORINTHIANS 13:2   *ten times*

If I have the gift of prophecy and understand all mysteries and all knowledge, and if I have all faith so that I can move mountains but do not have love, I am nothing.

1 Corinthians 13:2

RECITE 1 CORINTHIANS 13:2   *ten times*

WRITE OUT 1 CORINTHIANS 13:2
on the lines provided below

_____

_____

_____

_____

_____

_____

1 Corinthians 13:3

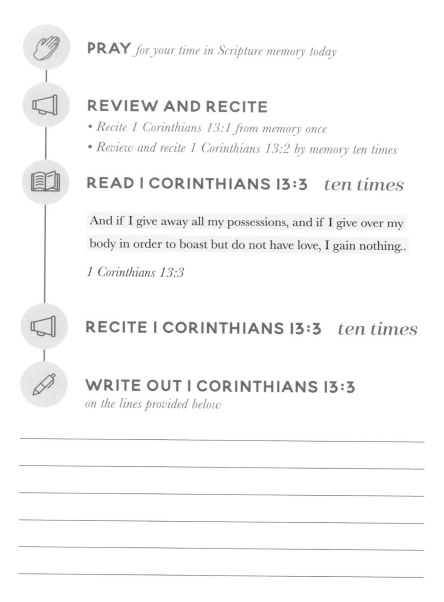

PRAY *for your time in Scripture memory today*

REVIEW AND RECITE
- Recite 1 Corinthians 13:1 from memory once
- Review and recite 1 Corinthians 13:2 by memory ten times

READ I CORINTHIANS 13:3 *ten times*

And if I give away all my possessions, and if I give over my body in order to boast but do not have love, I gain nothing..

1 Corinthians 13:3

RECITE I CORINTHIANS 13:3 *ten times*

WRITE OUT I CORINTHIANS 13:3
on the lines provided below

1 Corinthians 13:4

PRAY *for your time in Scripture memory today*

REVIEW AND RECITE
• *Recite 1 Corinthians 13:1-2 from memory once*
• *Review and recite 1 Corinthians 13:3 by memory ten times*

READ I CORINTHIANS 13:4 *ten times*

Love is patient, love is kind. Love does not envy, is not boastful, is not arrogant,

1 Corinthians 13:4

RECITE I CORINTHIANS 13:4 *ten times*

WRITE OUT I CORINTHIANS 13:4
on the lines provided below

_____

_____

_____

_____

_____

_____

1 Corinthians 13:5

PRAY *for your time in Scripture memory today*

REVIEW AND RECITE
- *Recite 1 Corinthians 13:1-3 from memory once*
- *Review and recite 1 Corinthians 13:4 by memory ten times*

READ I CORINTHIANS I3:5 *ten times*

is not rude, is not self-seeking, is not irritable,

and does not keep a record of wrongs.

1 Corinthians 13:5

RECITE I CORINTHIANS I3:5 *ten times*

WRITE OUT I CORINTHIANS I3:5
on the lines provided below

A Word Study

I CORINTHIANS 13

ἀγάπη

agapē

USED 116 TIMES
with variation

DEFINITION
love, typically referring to divine love

ἀγάπη

Agapē is the Greek word that translates in English to mean love, and more specifically, divine love. This is the variance of the word to describe the love that comes from God. It is used 116 times in the Bible with variation and is used nine times in the 1 Corinthians 13 passage.

As Christians, we know and understand love because we know God. He has shown the greatest act of love in the history of mankind by sending His one and only Son to pay the penalty for our sin so that we could be united with Him again—a love we could hardly fathom had we never experienced the life-transforming power of the gospel in our own lives. In that love, Christians now stand and are called to display God's great love to others.

1 Corinthians 13:6

PRAY *for your time in Scripture memory today*

REVIEW AND RECITE

• *Recite 1 Corinthians 13:1-4 from memory once*
• *Review and recite 1 Corinthians 13:5 by memory ten times*

READ I CORINTHIANS 13:6 *ten times*

Love finds no joy in unrighteousness
but rejoices in the truth.

1 Corinthians 13:6

RECITE I CORINTHIANS 13:6 *ten times*

WRITE OUT I CORINTHIANS 13:6
on the lines provided below

1 Corinthians 13:7

PRAY *for your time in Scripture memory today*

REVIEW AND RECITE
- *Recite 1 Corinthians 13:1-5 from memory once*
- *Review and recite 1 Corinthians 13:6 by memory ten times*

READ I CORINTHIANS I3:7 *ten times*

It bears all things, believes all things,

hopes all things, endures all things.

1 Corinthians 13:7

RECITE I CORINTHIANS I3:7 *ten times*

WRITE OUT I CORINTHIANS I3:7
on the lines provided below

1 Corinthians 13:8

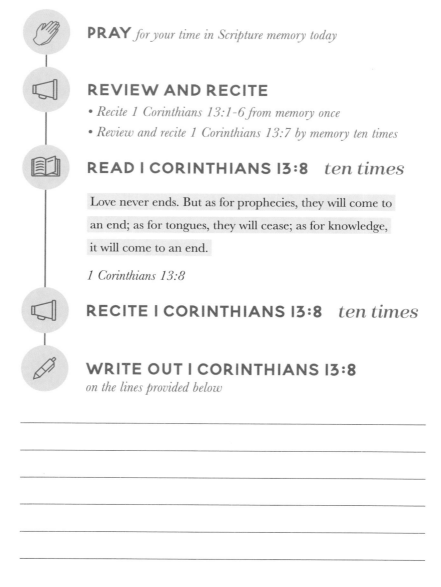

PRAY *for your time in Scripture memory today*

REVIEW AND RECITE
• *Recite 1 Corinthians 13:1-6 from memory once*
• *Review and recite 1 Corinthians 13:7 by memory ten times*

READ I CORINTHIANS 13:8   *ten times*

Love never ends. But as for prophecies, they will come to an end; as for tongues, they will cease; as for knowledge, it will come to an end.

1 Corinthians 13:8

RECITE I CORINTHIANS 13:8   *ten times*

WRITE OUT I CORINTHIANS 13:8
on the lines provided below

1 Corinthians 13:9

PRAY *for your time in Scripture memory today*

REVIEW AND RECITE
• *Recite 1 Corinthians 13:1-7 from memory once*
• *Review and recite 1 Corinthians 13:8 by memory ten times*

READ I CORINTHIANS 13:9 *ten times*

For we know in part, and we prophesy in part,

1 Corinthians 13:9

RECITE I CORINTHIANS 13:9 *ten times*

WRITE OUT I CORINTHIANS 13:9
on the lines provided below

1 Corinthians 13:10

PRAY *for your time in Scripture memory today*

REVIEW AND RECITE
• *Recite 1 Corinthians 13:1-8 from memory once*
• *Review and recite 1 Corinthians 13:9 by memory ten times*

READ I CORINTHIANS 13:10   *ten times*

but when the perfect comes,

the partial will come to an end.

1 Corinthians 13:10

RECITE I CORINTHIANS 13:10   *ten times*

WRITE OUT I CORINTHIANS 13:10
on the lines provided below

_____

_____

_____

_____

_____

_____

1 Corinthians 13:11

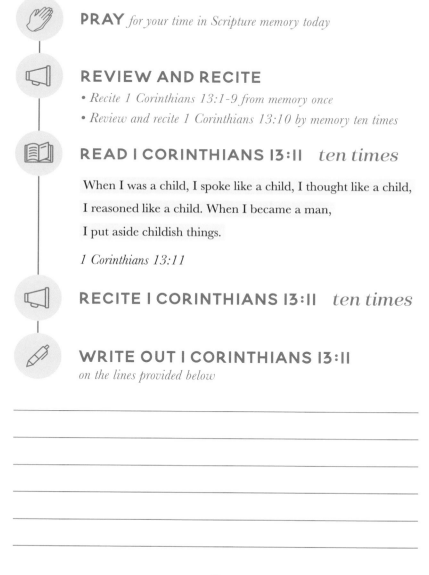

PRAY *for your time in Scripture memory today*

REVIEW AND RECITE
- *Recite 1 Corinthians 13:1-9 from memory once*
- *Review and recite 1 Corinthians 13:10 by memory ten times*

READ I CORINTHIANS 13:11   *ten times*

When I was a child, I spoke like a child, I thought like a child,

I reasoned like a child. When I became a man,

I put aside childish things.

1 Corinthians 13:11

RECITE I CORINTHIANS 13:11   *ten times*

WRITE OUT I CORINTHIANS 13:11
on the lines provided below

1 Corinthians 13:12

PRAY *for your time in Scripture memory today*

REVIEW AND RECITE
- *Recite 1 Corinthians 13:1-10 from memory once*
- *Review and recite 1 Corinthians 13:11 by memory ten times.*

READ I CORINTHIANS 13:12 *ten times*

For now we see only a reflection as in a mirror, but then face to face. Now I know in part, but then I will know fully, as I am fully known.

1 Corinthians 13:12

RECITE I CORINTHIANS 13:12 *ten times*

WRITE OUT I CORINTHIANS 13:12
on the lines provided below

1 Corinthians 13:13

PRAY *for your time in Scripture memory today*

REVIEW AND RECITE
- *Recite 1 Corinthians 13:1-11 from memory once*
- *Review and recite 1 Corinthians 13:12 by memory ten times*

READ I CORINTHIANS 13:13   *ten times*

Now these three remain: faith, hope, and love—
but the greatest of these is love.

1 Corinthians 13:13

RECITE I CORINTHIANS 13:13   *ten times*

WRITE OUT I CORINTHIANS 13:13
on the lines provided below

Conclusion

FOR I CORINTHIANS 13 SCRIPTURE MEMORY

WRITE OUT I CORINTHIANS 13 FROM MEMORY
on the lines provided below

_____

_____

_____

_____

_____

_____

_____

_____

_____

_____

_____

_____

_____

_____

_____

_____

_____

_____

_____

_____

_____

_____

_____

_____

_____

_____

_____

_____

_____

_____

_____

_____

_____

_____

_____

 PRAY *through the passage you have just memorized, thanking God for His character and how He has allowed you to study and dwell on His Word during this time.*

AN INTRO TO
The Armor of God
EPHESIANS 6:10-20

The Apostle Paul gives a strong picture of the spiritual war of Satan's opposition to God and His people in the portion of Scripture known as the Armor of God passages (Ephesians 6:10-20). It reminds us that we are living in a spiritual war, and apart from God's help, we are left defenseless. However, it also encourages Christians to utilize the weapons that God has provided for us to fight against the schemes of Satan. This passage informs us as to what our divine weapons are and how each is to serve us in the battle. God knew precisely how to equip us with weapons that would best defend ourselves and deploy the attacks of Satan.

As Christians, we can look to this passage with steady hope. At Jesus' first coming, He defeated sin and now has all rule, authority, power, and dominion (Ephesians 1:20-21). When Christ comes again, He will fully and finally defeat sin and Satan and deliver us completely. Though we are awaiting the final defeat of evil, and until that day, we can participate in Christ's victory now by trusting and relying on His strength and power. God has not left us to ourselves but prepares us daily for the battle. He equips us in every way we need to be equipped so that we can stand firm in the faith, unmoved, and awaiting glory.

Preparation

FOR MEMORIZING EPHESIANS 6:10-20

READ EPHESIANS 6:10-20

WRITE OUT EPHESIANS 6:10-20
on the lines provided below

_____

_____

_____

_____

_____

_____

_____

_____

_____

_____

_____

_____

_____

_____

_____

_____

_____

_____

_____

 PRAY *over the upcoming time you will spend memorizing and meditating on Ephesians 6:10-20*

Ephesians 6:10

PRAY *for your time in Scripture memory today*

READ EPHESIANS 6:10 *ten times*

Finally, be strengthened by the Lord
and by his vast strength.

Ephesians 6:10

RECITE EPHESIANS 6:10 *ten times*

WRITE OUT EPHESIANS 6:10
on the lines provided below

Ephesians 6:11

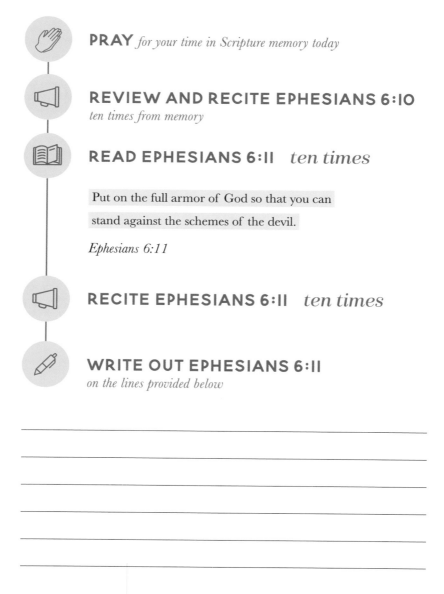

PRAY *for your time in Scripture memory today*

REVIEW AND RECITE EPHESIANS 6:10
ten times from memory

READ EPHESIANS 6:11 *ten times*

> Put on the full armor of God so that you can stand against the schemes of the devil.

Ephesians 6:11

RECITE EPHESIANS 6:11 *ten times*

WRITE OUT EPHESIANS 6:11
on the lines provided below

Ephesians 6:12

PRAY *for your time in Scripture memory today*

REVIEW AND RECITE
- *Recite Ephesians 6:10 from memory once*
- *Review and recite Ephesians 6:11 by memory ten times*

READ EPHESIANS 6:12 *ten times*

For our struggle is not against flesh and blood, but against the rulers, against the authorities, against the cosmic powers of this darkness, against evil, spiritual forces in the heavens.

Ephesians 6:12

RECITE EPHESIANS 6:12 *ten times*

WRITE OUT EPHESIANS 6:12
on the lines provided below

Ephesians 6:13

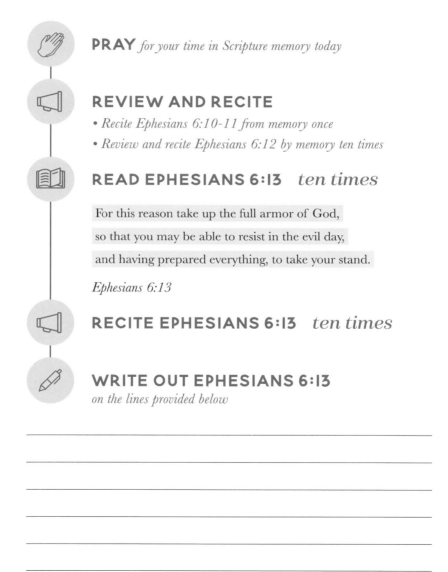

PRAY *for your time in Scripture memory today*

REVIEW AND RECITE
- *Recite Ephesians 6:10-11 from memory once*
- *Review and recite Ephesians 6:12 by memory ten times*

READ EPHESIANS 6:13   *ten times*

For this reason take up the full armor of God,

so that you may be able to resist in the evil day,

and having prepared everything, to take your stand.

Ephesians 6:13

RECITE EPHESIANS 6:13   *ten times*

WRITE OUT EPHESIANS 6:13
on the lines provided below

_____

_____

_____

_____

_____

_____

Ephesians 6:14

PRAY *for your time in Scripture memory today*

REVIEW AND RECITE
- *Recite Ephesians 6:10-12 from memory once*
- *Review and recite Ephesians 6:13 by memory ten times*

READ EPHESIANS 6:14 *ten times*

Stand, therefore, with truth like a belt around your waist, righteousness like armor on your chest,

Ephesians 6:14

RECITE EPHESIANS 6:14 *ten times*

WRITE OUT EPHESIANS 6:14
on the lines provided below

A Word Study

EPHESIANS 6:10-20

Πανοπλία

panoplia

 USED 3 TIMES

 DEFINITION
full, complete armor

Πανοπλία

Panoplia is the Greek word that translates in English to mean full armor or complete armor. It is used three times in the Bible and each time is presented in the context of gearing up for an attack. The hope of the Christian is that our armor cannot ever be taken from us. But this is nothing of our own doing. We are defenseless apart from the saving work of Jesus Christ. Our armor is complete because it is held by His ultimate strength and power. It does not rust, diminish, or loosen over time, but it will protect us all the way to glory. Therefore, we can confidently face each day with the assurance that God has given us everything we need for life and godliness, which includes weapons to defend the evil that haunts and tempts us. May we armor up each day clinging to our greatest help, because if God is for us, who can be against us!?

Ephesians 6:15

PRAY *for your time in Scripture memory today*

REVIEW AND RECITE
- *Recite Ephesians 6:10-13 from memory once*
- *Review and recite Ephesians 6:14 by memory ten times*

READ EPHESIANS 6:15 *ten times*

and your feet sandaled with readiness
for the gospel of peace.

Ephesians 6:15

RECITE EPHESIANS 6:15 *ten times*

WRITE OUT EPHESIANS 6:15
on the lines provided below

Ephesians 6:16

PRAY *for your time in Scripture memory today*

REVIEW AND RECITE
- *Recite Ephesians 6:10-14 from memory once*
- *Review and recite Ephesians 6:15 by memory ten times*

READ EPHESIANS 6:16 *ten times*

In every situation take up the shield of faith with which you can extinguish all the flaming arrows of the evil one.

Ephesians 6:16

RECITE EPHESIANS 6:16 *ten times*

WRITE OUT EPHESIANS 6:16
on the lines provided below

Ephesians 6:17

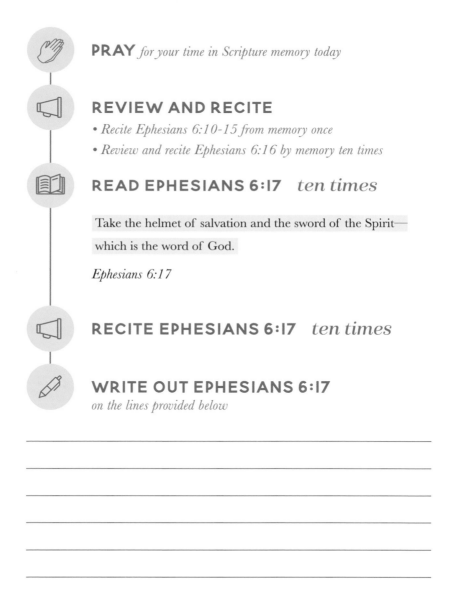

PRAY *for your time in Scripture memory today*

REVIEW AND RECITE
- *Recite Ephesians 6:10-15 from memory once*
- *Review and recite Ephesians 6:16 by memory ten times*

READ EPHESIANS 6:17 *ten times*

Take the helmet of salvation and the sword of the Spirit—
which is the word of God.

Ephesians 6:17

RECITE EPHESIANS 6:17 *ten times*

WRITE OUT EPHESIANS 6:17
on the lines provided below

_____

_____

_____

_____

_____

_____

Ephesians 6:18

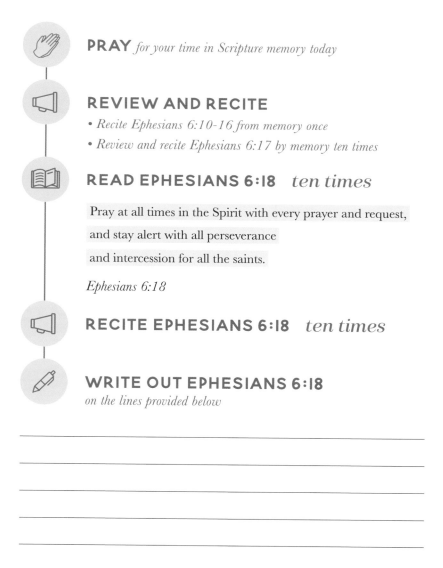

PRAY *for your time in Scripture memory today*

REVIEW AND RECITE
- *Recite Ephesians 6:10-16 from memory once*
- *Review and recite Ephesians 6:17 by memory ten times*

READ EPHESIANS 6:18 *ten times*

Pray at all times in the Spirit with every prayer and request, and stay alert with all perseverance and intercession for all the saints.

Ephesians 6:18

RECITE EPHESIANS 6:18 *ten times*

WRITE OUT EPHESIANS 6:18
on the lines provided below

Ephesians 6:19

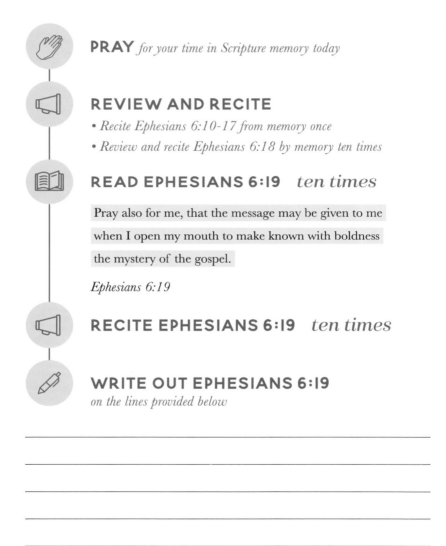

PRAY *for your time in Scripture memory today*

REVIEW AND RECITE
- *Recite Ephesians 6:10-17 from memory once*
- *Review and recite Ephesians 6:18 by memory ten times*

READ EPHESIANS 6:19 *ten times*

Pray also for me, that the message may be given to me when I open my mouth to make known with boldness the mystery of the gospel.

Ephesians 6:19

RECITE EPHESIANS 6:19 *ten times*

WRITE OUT EPHESIANS 6:19
on the lines provided below

_____

_____

_____

_____

_____

_____

Ephesians 6:20

PRAY *for your time in Scripture memory today*

REVIEW AND RECITE
- *Recite Ephesians 6:10-18 from memory once*
- *Review and recite Ephesians 6:19 by memory ten times*

READ EPHESIANS 6:20 *ten times*

For this I am an ambassador in chains. Pray that I might be bold enough to speak about it as I should.

Ephesians 6:20

RECITE EPHESIANS 6:20 *ten times*

WRITE OUT EPHESIANS 6:20
on the lines provided below

Conclusion

WRITE OUT EPHESIANS 6:10-20 FROM MEMORY
on the lines provided below

_____

_____

_____

_____

_____

_____

_____

_____

_____

_____

_____

_____

_____

_____

_____

_____

_____

_____

_____

_____

_____

_____

_____

_____

_____

_____

_____

_____

_____

_____

_____

_____

_____

_____

_____

_____

_____

 PRAY *through the passage you have just memorized, thanking God for His character and how He has allowed you to study and dwell on His Word during this time.*

AN INTRO TO
The Lord's Prayer
MATTHEW 6:5-15

The Lord's Prayer is one of the most recited and shared passages of Scripture among Christians. This prayer has been held in reverence since it was first spoken by Jesus Himself. Jesus shared this prayer with his disciples as a means of teaching, correcting, and modeling to them the important elements of prayer.

Entering into Matthew, we find the Lord's Prayer right in the middle of the Sermon on the Mount (Matthew 5-7). This sermon is given to set the tone that Jesus came to give us a righteousness that works its way all the way to our hearts and changes our attitudes. This perfectly prefaces the Lord's Prayer. There might be a temptation to approach prayer in a way that is robotic or outwardly pleasing, with our hearts and our attitude toward these practices unchanged.

Therefore, Jesus provides a rich foundational theology for prayer by presenting the strong example of the Lord's Prayer right in the middle of His corrective teaching. He reminds His disciples how we should pray and also highlights necessary requests and order to how we should pray. No one is better able to teach us these valuable elements and the true nature of prayer than Jesus Himself.

Preparation

FOR MEMORIZING MATTHEW 6:5-15

READ MATTHEW 6:5-15

WRITE OUT MATTHEW 6:5-15
on the lines provided below

_____

_____

_____

_____

_____

_____

_____

_____

_____

_____

_____

_____

_____

_____

_____

_____

_____

_____

_____

_____

_____

_____

_____

_____

_____

_____

_____

_____

_____

_____

_____

_____

_____

_____

_____

_____

PRAY *over the upcoming time you will spend memorizing and meditating on Matthew 6:5-15*

Matthew 6:5

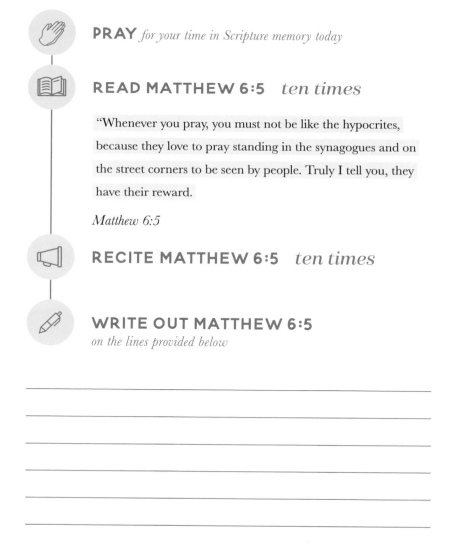

PRAY *for your time in Scripture memory today*

READ MATTHEW 6:5 *ten times*

"Whenever you pray, you must not be like the hypocrites, because they love to pray standing in the synagogues and on the street corners to be seen by people. Truly I tell you, they have their reward.

Matthew 6:5

RECITE MATTHEW 6:5 *ten times*

WRITE OUT MATTHEW 6:5
on the lines provided below

Matthew 6:6

PRAY *for your time in Scripture memory today*

REVIEW AND RECITE MATTHEW 6:5
ten times from memory

READ MATTHEW 6:6 *ten times*

But when you pray, go into your private room, shut your door, and pray to your Father who is in secret. And your Father who sees in secret will reward you.

Matthew 6:6

RECITE MATTHEW 6:6 *ten times*

WRITE OUT MATTHEW 6:6
on the lines provided below

_____

_____

_____

_____

_____

_____

Matthew 6:7

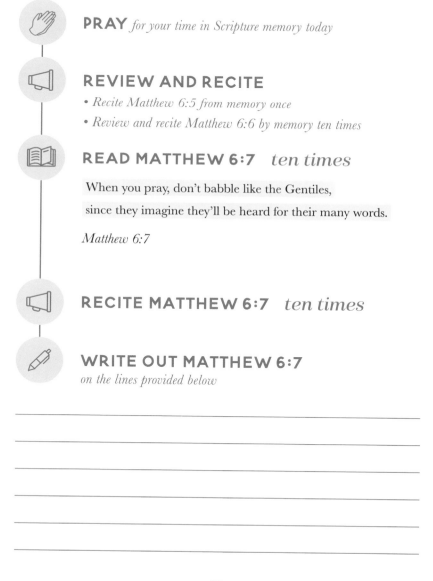

PRAY *for your time in Scripture memory today*

REVIEW AND RECITE
- *Recite Matthew 6:5 from memory once*
- *Review and recite Matthew 6:6 by memory ten times*

READ MATTHEW 6:7 *ten times*

When you pray, don't babble like the Gentiles,

since they imagine they'll be heard for their many words.

Matthew 6:7

RECITE MATTHEW 6:7 *ten times*

WRITE OUT MATTHEW 6:7
on the lines provided below

Matthew 6:8

PRAY *for your time in Scripture memory today*

REVIEW AND RECITE
- Recite Matthew 6:5-6 from memory once
- Review and recite Matthew 6:7 by memory ten times

READ MATTHEW 6:8 *ten times*

Don't be like them, because your Father knows the things you need before you ask him.

Matthew 6:8

RECITE MATTHEW 6:8 *ten times*

WRITE OUT MATTHEW 6:8
on the lines provided below

_____

_____

_____

_____

_____

_____

Matthew 6:9

PRAY *for your time in Scripture memory today*

REVIEW AND RECITE
- *Recite Matthew 6:5-7 from memory once*
- *Review and recite Matthew 6:8 by memory ten times*

READ MATTHEW 6:9 *ten times*

"Therefore, you should pray like this:

Our Father in heaven,

your name be honored as holy.

Matthew 6:9

RECITE MATTHEW 6:9 *ten times*

WRITE OUT MATTHEW 6:9
on the lines provided below

_____

_____

_____

_____

_____

_____

ἀγιάζω

---

hagiazō

USED 29 TIMES

DEFINITION
to make holy, consecrate, sanctify

ἁγιάζω

The Greek word *hagiazō* is translated into English meaning to make holy, consecrate, or sanctify. It is used 29 times in the Bible, one of which is used in the Lord's Prayer. It is found in the first petition in Matthew 6:9 which reads, "Therefore, you should pray like this: Our Father in heaven, your name be honored as holy." The order of this prayer begins with a request that God's name would be honored as holy. Jesus is calling us in prayer to worship God in His holiness by approaching Him in prayer with absolute reverence and considering His holy grandeur with every word, request, and thought in prayer. Additionally, our hearts are to be stirred for all people to know and revere God as holy, to worship and praise His name, and to enjoy Him now and forevermore. We are to pray to that end so that God will receive the honor and glory due His Name.

Matthew 6:10

PRAY *for your time in Scripture memory today*

REVIEW AND RECITE
- *Recite Matthew 6:5-8 from memory once*
- *Review and recite Matthew 6:9 by memory ten times*

READ MATTHEW 6:10   *ten times*

Your kingdom come.

Your will be done

on earth as it is in heaven.

Matthew 6:10

RECITE MATTHEW 6:10   *ten times*

WRITE OUT MATTHEW 6:10
on the lines provided below

Matthew 6:11

PRAY *for your time in Scripture memory today*

REVIEW AND RECITE
- *Recite Matthew 6:5-9 from memory once*
- *Review and recite Matthew 6:10 by memory ten times*

READ MATTHEW 6:11 *ten times*

Give us today our daily bread.

Matthew 6:11

RECITE MATTHEW 6:11 *ten times*

WRITE OUT MATTHEW 6:11
on the lines provided below

_____

_____

_____

_____

_____

_____

Matthew 6:12

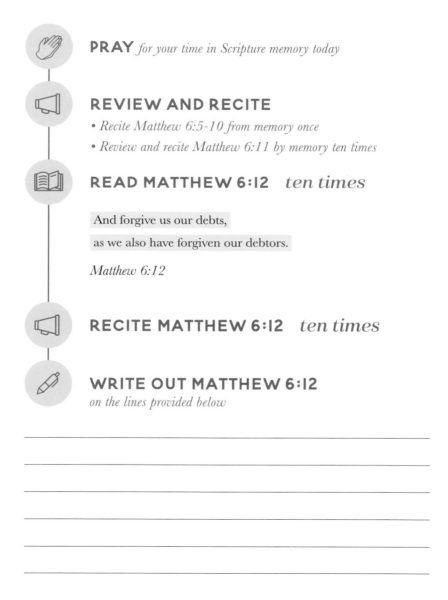

PRAY *for your time in Scripture memory today*

REVIEW AND RECITE
- *Recite Matthew 6:5-10 from memory once*
- *Review and recite Matthew 6:11 by memory ten times*

READ MATTHEW 6:12   *ten times*

And forgive us our debts,

as we also have forgiven our debtors.

Matthew 6:12

RECITE MATTHEW 6:12   *ten times*

WRITE OUT MATTHEW 6:12
on the lines provided below

_____

_____

_____

_____

_____

_____

Matthew 6:13

PRAY *for your time in Scripture memory today*

REVIEW AND RECITE
- *Recite Matthew 6:5-11 from memory once*
- *Review and recite Matthew 6:12 by memory ten times*

READ MATTHEW 6:13   *ten times*

And do not bring us into temptation,

but deliver us from the evil one.

Matthew 6:13

RECITE MATTHEW 6:13   *ten times*

WRITE OUT MATTHEW 6:13
on the lines provided below

_____

_____

_____

_____

_____

_____

Matthew 6:14

PRAY *for your time in Scripture memory today*

REVIEW AND RECITE
• *Recite Matthew 6:5-12 from memory once*
• *Review and recite Matthew 6:13 by memory ten times*

READ MATTHEW 6:14 *ten times*

"For if you forgive others their offenses,

your heavenly Father will forgive you as well.

Matthew 6:14

RECITE MATTHEW 6:14 *ten times*

WRITE OUT MATTHEW 6:14
on the lines provided below

_____

_____

_____

_____

_____

_____

Matthew 6:15

PRAY *for your time in Scripture memory today*

REVIEW AND RECITE
- *Recite Matthew 6:5-13 from memory once*
- *Review and recite Matthew 6:14 by memory ten times*

READ MATTHEW 6:15 *ten times*

But if you don't forgive others, your Father will not forgive your offenses.

Matthew 6:15

RECITE MATTHEW 6:15 *ten times*

WRITE OUT MATTHEW 6:15
on the lines provided below

_____

_____

_____

_____

_____

_____

Conclusion

WRITE OUT MATTHEW 6:5-15 FROM MEMORY
on the lines provided below

_____

_____

_____

_____

_____

_____

_____

_____

_____

_____

_____

_____

_____

_____

_____

_____

_____

_____

_____

_____

_____

_____

_____

_____

_____

_____

_____

_____

_____

_____

_____

_____

_____

_____

_____

 PRAY *through the passage you have just memorized, thanking God for His character and how He has allowed you to study and dwell on His Word during this time.*

AN INTRO TO
The Fruit of the Spirit
GALATIANS 5:16-26

Galatians 5 begins by calling Christians to live in light of the freedom they have been given through Christ to love and serve one another. Paul's words in Galatians 5:16-26 exhort Christians to do so by living in the Spirit. By the power of the Spirit, new life in Christ gives us continued assurance of the presence of the Spirit to lead and guide us in faithful obedience. We no longer are ruled by the ways of the flesh but instead cling to the hope of the Spirit at work in us. Therefore, we are empowered to put off the desires of the flesh listed but not limited to sexual immorality, moral impurity, promiscuity, idolatry, sorcery, hatreds, strife, jealousy, outbursts of anger, selfish ambitions, dissensions, factions, envy, drunkenness, carousing, and anything similar. We are set free to walk by the Spirit and to practically see the fruit of the Spirit produced in our lives.

This passage lists nine specific characteristics revealed in our lives as a result of the Holy Spirit. The fruit listed is love, joy, peace, patience, kindness, generosity, faithfulness, gentleness, and self-control. These characteristics are in opposition to the ways of the flesh, but as we walk in the ways of the Spirit, we will see the fruit of it evidenced in our lives. We will grow in love, patience, and kindness toward one another. We will grow in gentleness and self-control when provoked by our circumstances. We will grow in faithfulness to the work we have been called to. We will grow in generosity with what we have been given. We will grow in peace that surpasses all understanding. And we will grow in overflowing joy that anchors securely in our salvation. The fruit of the Spirit at work in us is profound evidence of God's care for His people. We are reminded of that truth through this passage that we have been given the help of His Spirit along the way to equip us, shape us into the likeness of Christ, and prepare us for heaven.

READ GALATIANS 5:16-26

WRITE OUT GALATIANS 5:16-26
on the lines provided below

_____

_____

_____

_____

_____

_____

_____

_____

_____

_____

_____

_____

_____

_____

_____

_____

_____

_____

_____

_____

_____

_____

_____

_____

_____

_____

_____

_____

_____

_____

_____

_____

_____

_____

_____

 PRAY *over the upcoming time you will spend memorizing and meditating on Galatians 5:16-26*

Galatians 5:16

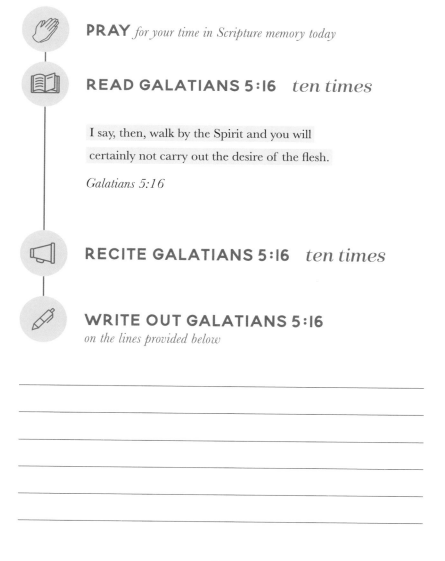

PRAY *for your time in Scripture memory today*

READ GALATIANS 5:16 *ten times*

> I say, then, walk by the Spirit and you will
> certainly not carry out the desire of the flesh.

Galatians 5:16

RECITE GALATIANS 5:16 *ten times*

WRITE OUT GALATIANS 5:16
on the lines provided below

Galatians 5:17

PRAY *for your time in Scripture memory today*

REVIEW AND RECITE GALATIANS 5:16
ten times from memory

READ GALATIANS 5:17   *ten times*

For the flesh desires what is against the Spirit, and the Spirit desires what is against the flesh; these are opposed to each other, so that you don't do what you want.

Galatians 5:17

RECITE GALATIANS 5:17   *ten times*

WRITE OUT GALATIANS 5:17
on the lines provided below

Galatians 5:18

PRAY *for your time in Scripture memory today*

REVIEW AND RECITE

- *Recite Galatians 5:16 from memory once*
- *Review and recite Galatians 5:17 by memory ten times*

READ GALATIANS 5:18 *ten times*

But if you are led by the Spirit, you are not under the law.

Galatians 5:18

RECITE GALATIANS 5:18 *ten times*

WRITE OUT GALATIANS 5:18
on the lines provided below

Galatians 5:19

PRAY *for your time in Scripture memory today*

REVIEW AND RECITE

- *Recite Galatians 5:16-17 from memory once*
- *Review and recite Galatians 5:18 by memory ten times*

READ GALATIANS 5:19 *ten times*

Now the works of the flesh are obvious: sexual immorality, moral impurity, promiscuity,

Galatians 5:19

RECITE GALATIANS 5:19 *ten times*

WRITE OUT GALATIANS 5:19
on the lines provided below

Galatians 5:20

PRAY *for your time in Scripture memory today*

REVIEW AND RECITE
- *Recite Galatians 5:16-18 from memory once*
- *Review and recite Galatians 5:19 by memory ten times*

READ GALATIANS 5:20 *ten times*

idolatry, sorcery, hatreds, strife, jealousy, outbursts of anger, selfish ambitions, dissensions, factions,

Galatians 5:20

RECITE GALATIANS 5:20 *ten times*

WRITE OUT GALATIANS 5:20
on the lines provided below

A Word Study

GALATIANS 5:16-26

καρπός

karpos

USED 66 TIMES

DEFINITION
fruit, the product of

καρπός

The Greek word *karpos* is translated in English to mean fruit or product of something. The word is found to be used both literally and figuratively in the Bible. It seems to be mostly used figuratively—41 times to be exact. When we see this word used figuratively, it often speaks of spiritual fruit or evidence of the power of Christ at work through His people. This spiritual fruit represents the true, changed motivations and affections of the heart through actions and attitudes.

We find examples of these differing fruits, whether spiritual or not, when Paul speaks of the fruit of the Spirit in Galatians 5:19-23. Evidence of life in Christ is produced through motivations, affections, actions, and attitudes. Our lives will bear the fruit of something—the flesh or the Spirit. So may we choose to "walk worthy of the Lord, fully pleasing to him: bearing fruit in every good work and growing in the knowledge of God" (Colossians 1:10) so that our lives will demonstrate evidence of God's good and faithful work in us.

Galatians 5:21

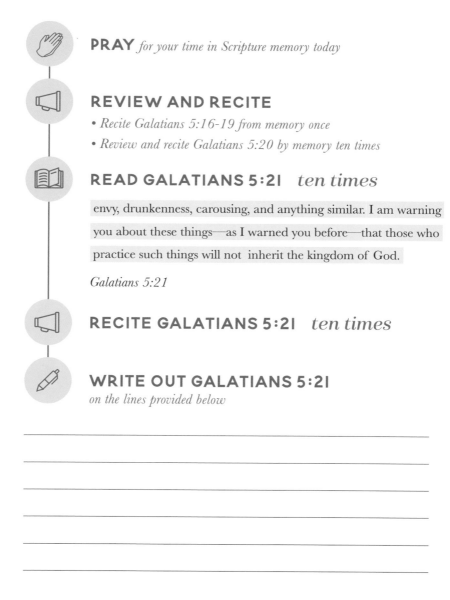

PRAY *for your time in Scripture memory today*

REVIEW AND RECITE
- *Recite Galatians 5:16-19 from memory once*
- *Review and recite Galatians 5:20 by memory ten times*

READ GALATIANS 5:21 *ten times*

envy, drunkenness, carousing, and anything similar. I am warning you about these things—as I warned you before—that those who practice such things will not inherit the kingdom of God.

Galatians 5:21

RECITE GALATIANS 5:21 *ten times*

WRITE OUT GALATIANS 5:21
on the lines provided below

_____

_____

_____

_____

_____

_____

Galatians 5:22

PRAY *for your time in Scripture memory today*

REVIEW AND RECITE
- *Recite Galatians 5:16-20 from memory once*
- *Review and recite Galatians 5:21 by memory ten times*

READ GALATIANS 5:22 *ten times*

But the fruit of the Spirit is love, joy, peace, patience, kindness, goodness, faithfulness,

Galatians 5:22

RECITE GALATIANS 5:22 *ten times*

WRITE OUT GALATIANS 5:22
on the lines provided below

Galatians 5:23

PRAY *for your time in Scripture memory today*

REVIEW AND RECITE
- *Recite Galatians 5:16-21 from memory once*
- *Review and recite Galatians 5:22 by memory ten times*

READ GALATIANS 5:23   *ten times*

gentleness, and self-control.

The law is not against such things.

Galatians 5:23

RECITE GALATIANS 5:23   *ten times*

WRITE OUT GALATIANS 5:23
on the lines provided below

Galatians 5:24

PRAY *for your time in Scripture memory today*

REVIEW AND RECITE
• *Recite Galatians 5:16-22 from memory once*
• *Review and recite Galatians 5:23 by memory ten times*

READ GALATIANS 5:24 *ten times*

Now those who belong to Christ Jesus have crucified the flesh with its passions and desires.

Galatians 5:24

RECITE GALATIANS 5:24 *ten times*

WRITE OUT GALATIANS 5:24
on the lines provided below

Galatians 5:25

PRAY *for your time in Scripture memory today*

REVIEW AND RECITE
- *Recite Galatians 5:16-23 from memory once*
- *Review and recite Galatians 5:24 by memory ten times*

READ GALATIANS 5:25 *ten times*

If we live by the Spirit, let us also keep in step with the Spirit.

Galatians 5:25

RECITE GALATIANS 5:25 *ten times*

WRITE OUT GALATIANS 5:25
on the lines provided below

_____

_____

_____

_____

_____

_____

Galatians 5:26

PRAY *for your time in Scripture memory today*

REVIEW AND RECITE
- *Recite Galatians 5:16-24 from memory once*
- *Review and recite Galatians 5:25 by memory ten times*

READ GALATIANS 5:26   *ten times*

Let us not become conceited, provoking
one another, envying one another.

Galatians 5:26

RECITE GALATIANS 5:26   *ten times*

WRITE OUT GALATIANS 5:26
on the lines provided below

Conclusion

FOR GALATIANS 5:16-26 SCRIPTURE MEMORY

WRITE OUT GALATIANS 5:16-26 FROM MEMORY
on the lines provided below

_____

_____

_____

_____

_____

_____

_____

_____

_____

_____

_____

_____

_____

_____

_____

_____

_____

_____

_____

_____

_____

_____

_____

_____

_____

_____

_____

_____

_____

_____

_____

_____

_____

_____

_____

_____

_____

_____

_____

_____

 PRAY *through the passage you have just memorized, thanking God for His character and how He has allowed you to study and dwell on His Word during this time.*

AN INTRO TO
The Great Commission
MATTHEW 28:18-20

Matthew 28:18-20 is the passage well-known as the Great Commission. After Jesus' resurrection, He gathered His disciples in Galilee on a mountain. The words spoken by Jesus served as a departing message. He began by telling His disciples that all authority in heaven and on earth had been given to Him. Paul expounds on this in Colossians 1:16-20 saying, "For everything was created by him, in heaven and on earth, the visible and the invisible, whether thrones or dominions or rulers or authorities—all things have been created through him and for him. He is before all things, and by him all things hold together. He is also the head of the body, the church; he is the beginning, the firstborn from the dead, so that he might come to have first place in everything. For God was pleased to have all his fullness dwell in him, and through him to reconcile everything to himself, whether things on earth or things in heaven, by making peace through his blood, shed on the cross."

With that power and authority given by God, He commands, or commissions, His disciples to go out into the world to continue sharing the good news of the gospel to all who will listen. The hope and aim of sharing the gospel is that many will come to know Jesus as their Lord and Savior, being baptized into the faith and trained up as a disciple. Additionally, Jesus gives His disciples the authority to teach others in His name with what they have been entrusted with. This is a privileged and purposeful command given to the disciples, essentially, to continue the work of Jesus until He returns.

The Great Commission is not only a command for the first disciples but a command for every Christian. Just as we have heard the good news of the gospel, so we are to be faithful to share it until Jesus returns. We have been equipped in every way to continue making disciples of every nation. Jesus does not command and send out without a promise. Jesus' closing words as He draws nearer to His ascension to heaven is that He will be with His people always to the end of the ages. We are not left to ourselves, our own words, and our own efforts. Instead, we are prepped for His work with the promise of Jesus' continued presence in our lives. We have no reason to be afraid or ashamed, for He will be with us every step of the way— helping us, comforting us, equipping us, and preparing us for His gospel work. We can remain faithful to this commission with ultimate hope—that Jesus is calling people to Himself and has invited us to be a part of that work.

.

Preparation

 READ MATTHEW 28:18-20

 WRITE OUT MATTHEW 28:18-20
on the lines provided below

_____

_____

_____

_____

_____

_____

_____

_____

_____

_____

_____

_____

_____

_____

_____

_____

_____

_____

_____

_____

_____

_____

_____

_____

_____

_____

_____

_____

_____

_____

_____

_____

_____

_____

_____

_____

_____

 PRAY *over the upcoming time you will spend memorizing and meditating on Matthew 28:18-20*

Matthew 28:18

PRAY *for your time in Scripture memory today*

READ MATTHEW 28:18   *ten times*

Jesus came near and said to them, "All authority has been given to me in heaven and on earth.

Matthew 28:18

RECITE MATTHEW 28:18   *ten times*

WRITE OUT MATTHEW 28:18
on the lines provided below

Matthew 28:19

PRAY *for your time in Scripture memory today*

REVIEW AND RECITE MATTHEW 28:18
ten times from memory

READ MATTHEW 28:19 *ten times*

Go, therefore, and make disciples of all nations, baptizing them in the name of the Father and of the Son and of the Holy Spirit,

Matthew 28:19

RECITE MATTHEW 28:19 *ten times*

WRITE OUT MATTHEW 28:19
on the lines provided below

ἐξουσία

exousia

USED 102 TIMES

DEFINITION
the power to act, authority

ἐξουσία

The Greek word *exousia* is translated into English as the power to act, or authority. It is used 102 times in the Bible with variation. In the New Testament, this word refers to the authority given by God to His saints, authorizing them to act in response to His revealed Word. The Bible reminds us that authority begins with God the Father, is revealed through the Son, is manifested by the Holy Spirit, and is revealed through the Word to the church and the world. God's people are given this authority by God to serve in faith and to build up the church. We see this exemplified in God's commission to His disciples and the command of the Bible. By faith, we are to cling to the authority of Scripture, and we can confidently obey out of deep and devoted love for the Lord.

Matthew 28:20

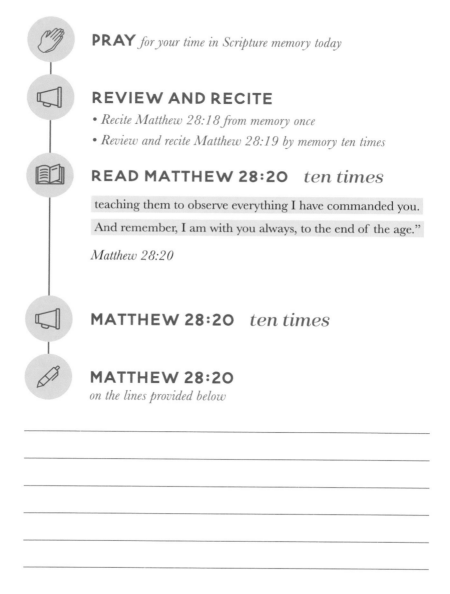

PRAY *for your time in Scripture memory today*

REVIEW AND RECITE
- *Recite Matthew 28:18 from memory once*
- *Review and recite Matthew 28:19 by memory ten times*

READ MATTHEW 28:20 *ten times*

teaching them to observe everything I have commanded you. And remember, I am with you always, to the end of the age."

Matthew 28:20

MATTHEW 28:20 *ten times*

MATTHEW 28:20
on the lines provided below

Conclusion

FOR MATTHEW 28:18-20 SCRIPTURE MEMORY

WRITE OUT MATTHEW 28:18-20 FROM MEMORY
on the lines provided below

_____

_____

_____

_____

_____

_____

_____

_____

_____

_____

_____

_____

_____

_____

_____

_____

_____

_____

_____

_____

 PRAY *through the passage you have just memorized, thanking God for His character and how He has allowed you to study and dwell on His Word during this time.*

FOR STUDYING GOD'S
WORD WITH US!

CONNECT WITH US:

@THEDAILYGRACECO

@KRISTINSCHMUCKER

CONTACT US:

INFO@THEDAILYGRACECO.COM

SHARE:

#THEDAILYGRACECO

#LAMPANDLIGHT

WEBSITE:

WWW.THEDAILYGRACECO.COM